FIFTY ONE SHADES OF SELFIES - IT'S SELFIE TIME!

THE ULTIMATE BUCKET LIST

GUIDEBOOK

What are YOU really trying to show and reveal about yourself?

SID ALI SABIR

Copyright

CONTENTS

A must have tool for all you selfie takers

The Revelation

When we take certain selfies what are we really trying to show and reveal about ourselves?

This guidebook has been written in good fun and to explore why we actually take different types of selfies. There are many Apps and websites where we all go on to share certain pictures we have just taken that are sometimes seen by complete strangers. Are we trying to say something more about ourselves does a picture say a thousand words? I happen to think there truly is a hidden message that we are secretly and sometimes obviously conveying.

People take selfies without truly thinking about what it actually says about them as a person. When you take a selfie and send it out into the digital world the chances are it will be seen by other people who might not know you well enough. You may have sent a selfie to a friend who then re-sends it to another friend. Or you could be a prolific user of the many social media networking platforms out there today. Once that selfie is out there it is then pretty much out of your hands and in the hands of others. This guidebook will help open your eyes to what you might be portraying about yourself. A selfie can make you look worse off or portray you as something else to others, as they might be reading you as a certain type of individual. This guidebook will help you read a person better and reveal to you what an individual might actually be saying about themselves. It will help you equip yourself with the knowledge to have the power over your own selfies, so you can truly be in control with the image and statement you want to send out to the world.

I personally haven't latched onto the selfie craze and I am a bit late coming into it. I have seen many selfies that people don't mind sharing to complete strangers and wondered why they had the need to share a certain selfie. I find myself a little reluctant in sharing aspects of myself and my life. Some people send a variety of different types of selfies in various poses and of different things. Whereas others like me send out plenty of the same type of selfies. I wondered if the selfies I was sharing put me in any sort of category and what did it say about me as a person.

This guidebook will reveal around 51 types of selfies I have come across and I will try to reveal what I think a certain type of selfie is **inadvertently** revealing about the person taking that certain selfie. The guidebook will expose FOUR types of Selfie categories:
- 1 Beginner / 2 Transitional / 3 Advance / 4 Extreme

The more we share ourselves through the different shades of selfies the more likely we are to explore ourselves further through a variety of selfies. Moving with ease through the identified categories as the selfie lifestyle becomes the norm and we inadvertently expose our true selves evermore.

The Selfies this guidebook refer to are the type of pictures we shoot and send out to friends or onto popular Apps or websites. It does not mean that you have to be in the picture. As the selfie is taken and sent off by the individual, this guidebook will help you expose what the selfie taker is really possibly and most likely showcasing about themselves.

Read on and have fun!

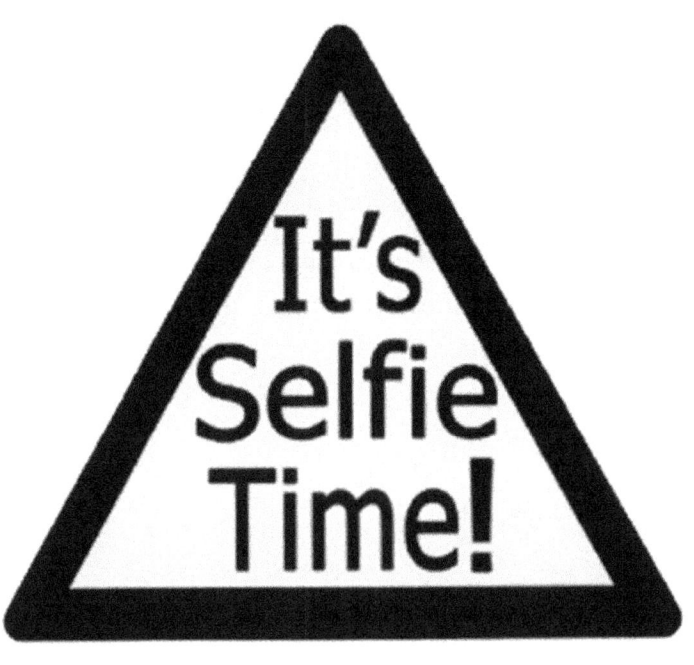

1 SELFIES - FOR BEGINNERS

1.   Pictures of Food

Not too comfortable with sharing a lot about yourself yet but comfortable enough to show your likes or dislikes of certain food. You're still a pretty much private person who is very controlling and a bit shy.

2.   Notes and statements

Expressing yourself in a safe way where you feel comfortable to let others know a bit more about you and your thoughts, opinions and possibly your stance on things. You have an inspirational side which is emerging.

3.   Pictures of Buildings

Possibly conveying your reluctance to be seen but wanting to be seen somewhat interesting and that you have a lively side so you don't come across boring.

4.   Posing with food

Trying to get comfortable to the ideas of selfies and revealing yourself to others. Without it screaming out that you want attention. You are a composed but sensitive person.

5.   Food rearranged

Showing your playful and hilarious side through depicting your food to represent something else. You are releasing your inner child.

6.   Posing in front of Buildings

Coming out of your shell and showing that you are someone who is going places in life. You have ambitions and like to explore.

7.   Natural look

Most people start their selfie life comfortable in their normal essence, to show off their natural daily look. A strong statement that says this is me. You are carefree and have a lot of pride.

8.   Mirror poses

Getting that look just right and practising it in the mirror. You almost have full confidence in yourself as you are in full control of your own image. Taking a selfie in front of a mirror and not relying on others to take it, shows some reluctant or lack of confidence within yourself to trust others yet. Or simply no one was around so you improvised. You have a playful side to you.

9.   Random self poses

Pictures doing random things from your daily life such as watching TV, reading a book, playing sports etc. You are impulsive, expressing yourself in a positive way and showing others you are comfortable in letting them into your world.

10.   With friends

You have built the confidence and are very comfortable to show how you share your life with others who are close to you. You have a sentimental side and a trusting nature and can be very protective.

2 SELFIES - Transitional

11.   Cute Baby

Contentment in showing you have a sensitive, affectionate and caring side and want others to appreciate the cute baby shot just as much as you did.

12.   Images of pets

You are easily excited and get attached to things. You are comfortable to show you have a sensitive and or comedic side and share the other loved ones you have in your family. Want others to appreciate your pets or that funny, silly shot captured in that moment. You have a very giving side to you and you want others to see and to feel that warmth, fun and happiness too.

13.   Posing with pets or wildlife

You just can't help yourself being in that shot. It screams out 'look at me I'm with animals and I respect nature too. Like the pet like me too?'

14.   Sleeping

Haa haa someone got you while you were sleeping. Shows you are not too concerned about what others see even when you are at your most vulnerable state.

15.   Pouting

You don't mind showing that odd pose that tries to say 'kiss me I'm feeling sexy today, check me out.'

16. With family

Very secure and comfortable about yourself. You are totally fine to let others see the extended side of your private life. You are a person who appreciates and is thankful for what they have in life.

17. Fancy vehicles

Something caught your eye as you were passing by that you appreciated so much and you just had to share it with others. So they can experience that WOW moment (Very kind of you to do so). You crave and long for something more to come into your life.

18. Posing with impressive vehicles

In most cases you managed to sneak a pose and just had to brag to others hoping they think it was yours. Or possibly you have an arsenal of posh vehicles that you just want to show off. You are amused and impressed very easily.

19.   With partner

Comfortable in your relationship and happy to let others know this about you. You have a strong bond and you send out the message hands off I'm taken. You are affectionate and a romantic person someone who appreciates the finer things in life.

20.   At work

The other side of your life. You are very sharing and don't mind others seeing you at the place you spend a good proportion of time of your daily life.

Good or bad times you have got that selfie bug and need to vent out or share that moment. Showing you are an achiever and hardworking go getter.

Basically letting others know you got a job and money coming in.

3 SELFIES - ADVANCE

21.   Kissing partner

Happy and comfortable in your relationship and you just want to show how much in love you really are. You are a very romantic and sentimental person.

22.   Silly / Prankster

The mischievous side of you has come out and you need to let others know that they have to watch out for you. It also shows you don't take yourself too serious and you're not bothered who else sees you looking silly or doing something silly. You're a cheerful and fun person to be around but mostly an attention seeker.

23.   Almost nude body shot

Feeling good about yourself and have confidence to show yourself exposed but not too compromised. You are seductive, brave and daring and you want others to appreciate what you have. That shirtless, bikini shot, almost revealing half covered up, bicep or six pack shot, come on you all know the ones I'm talking about. You have certain desires and secretly crave for something more.

You want people to admire you and seek appreciation.

24.   Alone intense looking

You're a natural Selfie taker and you know how to make it count. You are in full control of that perfect shot that shows the emotion off just right. You have a habit of exposing your different sides and you just need to share it to expose yourself. You are quite mischievous, composed and a reflective person

25.   All dolled up

Looking your best - make up check / clothes check / jewellery or accessories check / Snap the shots taken and wow the love and appreciation keeps coming back. It's the million dollar shot and of course you are going to share it. You seek admiration and it's good to be vain at times we all need that pat on the back or that compliment.

It also says 'check me out now damn I'm looking fine, you know you want me.'

26. At the gym

You have worked hard and it's a good reminder to yourself and others what hard work could help you achieve. Your work ethic and determination shines through so of course you need to share it. To say the least you are self-alert, energetic and a positive individual.

27. Strange objects

You can get fascinated over things and your inquisitive side is being shared and by now you don't mind sharing anything that comes to mind.

28. Posing with a musical instrument

Besides saying 'look at me rocking it.' You are trying to show there's more to you as a person depending on the instrument. Whether you can play or not? Well it's a selfie, so who's going to know. You are yearning for challenges to come your way.

29. Family events

You are a very affectionate person who is sentimental and you put trust in others very quickly.

A very personal moments being shared. Your life and loved ones caught in a moment in time. Happiness overcomes you and you need to show that epic moment so it is for ever more. You want to let others in to be a part of your life during the happy times.

30. On the toilet

It happens. You're bored and your fingers are twitching so you take that shot and share it with a few close friends. You have confidence in abundance and can laugh at yourself with others. You are very playful, mischievous, friendly and easily excited.

4 EXTREME SELFIES - SHOW OFF

31. Bags, watches, shoes and tat

If you got it flaunt it. It is what it is. You want your possessions to be appreciated by others, you truly are a giving person. You form an attachment to things very quickly

32. Posing inside impressive vehicles

Mainly a guy thing someone with an ego. Want to say 'look at me it's all about me and what I have. I own this and hopefully I'll get a lot of chicks from it.' Full of testosterone and attention seeking (Of course I may be wrong)

33. Events/holidays

You appreciate things, like surprises a lot and are an active person. Yes you have been somewhere it screams 'look at me now I'm having fun wish you were here too? My life is full of fun.'

The odd holiday shot is not showing off, but too many holidays in a year, I think it's called bragging. However the other side to it is you might have had a nightmare of a time and you may be warning others and that's a very noble thing.

34.   In your very Best expensive clothes

We know who you are you superstars you…

Totally bragging and showing off every day looking there absolute best. You want appreciation some ass kissing comments, mainly positive ones nonstop. You just scream out 'appreciate me now and forever.' You are an affectionate person who has plenty of passion, pride and confidence and let's not forget a big ego.

35.   With famous people

Hey look who I'm with! Need to brag and boast to look good (a well-connected person - REALLY).

36.   In the Bath / Shower

The odd one is fine if it's tastily done. Otherwise it yells out 'follow me, appreciate me and look how amazing I am' (Someone's getting very vain). You are a passionate person who has desires and craves for some excitement.

37.   During sex

Please do we really need to see that? Mostly a private shot that should be kept that way and a personal memory. If it's going out to the public than damn you got some explaining to do (It happens). You are a very intimate and sensual person, who is energetic and easy-going,

38.   After sex

That boasting shot looking tired and to say you just done the deed. (Keep it to yourself will you). You are a keen person who reflects on things. You like to seek approval and assurance from others.

39.   Fully nude body shot

Plenty of these around. If you got it flaunt it and show it off. You have too much self believe and confidence nothing can bring you down and you just want to share your beauty to the world to see. There is the possibility you enjoy winding others up as a result. You have a very playful and carefree side.

40.   Sexy body posing

You're just a flirt flaunting your assets for admiration. You have an insecure side too and you seek attention.

41.   PhotoShopped

Done correctly it's for fun and laughs. Can show lack of confidence, insecurity and fakeness if you are using it to improve your bits if you know what I mean. You're trying hard to please and impress.

42.   With loads of Money

You got it but do you really need to pose with it (ego alert). Totally vain and a show off need I explain the motive any more.

43.   In a plane 1st class

Doing social work letting others see parts of the good life being enjoyed. It could be a treasured moment and you are exhilarated and jubilant. You want to send out a statement that you have made it.

44.   In a 5 star posh hotel room

Again doing social work and letting people in to see a privileged lifestyle. Admittedly it's the norm for the selfie taker but for the masses it's showing off. It says you enjoy the finer life and anything less is beneath you.

45.   Model pose

You look good anyway but you can't stop yourself you just have to try out a professional model pose. You see yourself nothing less than a model and too right you go for it and work it. Let the world see you working it. You seek for affection and attention.

46.   Posing with actual Models

Yes it's a lottery ticket to getting the bragging rights. You got the shot, now time to get others jealous.

47.   With dangerous wildlife

You're either brave or stupid? You're a thrill seeker who is fascinated and jubilant. You're saying you can take it to the next level and you have no fear.

48. Under water

Your brave and love to explore. You love nature and somewhat like to be at the centre of attention. You're saying you have got some big ones and you've done something special. You like to try out new things.

49. In Space

The ultimate selfie maybe in the future or if you can afford it. Only a handful of astronauts can claim this bragging right. This selfie screams out 'I'm too extreme beat that if you can.'

THE RARE SELFIES

The human in us all comes out now and again. There's not many of these selfies around as they do change the mood. We take many selfies of certain aspects of life which paints a picture that's positive. We rarely show our own faults and our downsides as it comes down to being defensive. I find that I cannot categories these types of selfies.

50. Accident/incident

Capturing and sharing as a warning or to highlight the sadness. Showing your caring nature i.e. motherly, fatherly, big brother or sisterly side. You have compassion and affection towards others.

51. Poor and destitute

Capturing and sharing to highlight a cause or the sadness. You have compassion are friendly and the sensitive side shows your caring nature i.e. motherly, fatherly, big brother or sisterly side.

THE LIST - 51 SHADES OF SELFIES

Beginners

1. Pictures of Food ☐
2. Notes and statements ☐
3. Pictures of Buildings ☐
4. Posing with food ☐
5. Food rearranged ☐
6. Posing in front of Buildings ☐
7. Natural look ☐
8. Mirror poses ☐
9. Random self poses ☐
10. With friends ☐

Transitional

11. Cute Baby ☐
12. Images of pets ☐
13. Posing with pets or wildlife ☐
14. Sleeping ☐
15. Pouting ☐
16. With family ☐
17. Fancy vehicles ☐
18. Posing with impressive vehicles ☐

19.	With partner	☐
20.	At work	☐

Advance

21.	Kissing partner	☐
22.	Silly / Prankster	☐
23.	Almost nude body shot	☐
24.	Alone intense looking	☐
25.	All dolled up	☐
26.	At the gym	☐
27.	Strange objects	☐
28.	Posing with a musical instrument	☐
29.	Family events	☐
30.	On the toilet	☐

Extreme Selfies -Show Off

31.	Bags, watches, shoes and tat	☐
32.	Posing inside impressive vehicles	☐
33.	Events/holidays	☐
34.	In your very Best expensive clothes	☐
35.	With famous people	☐
36.	In the Bath / Shower	☐
37.	During sex	☐
38.	After sex	☐

39.	Fully nude body shot	☐
40.	Sexy body posing	☐
41.	PhotoShopped	☐
42.	With loads of Money	☐
43.	In a plane 1st class	☐
44.	In a 5 star posh hotel room	☐
45.	Model pose	☐
46.	Posing with actual Models	☐
47.	With dangerous wildlife	☐
48.	Under Water	☐
49.	In Space	☐

Rare

| 50. | Accident/incident | ☐ |
| 51. | Poor and destitute | ☐ |

> ➢ **Why don't you compare and tally up to see how many types of selfies you have sent to see which category you might come under. To achieve the higher category you need to have completed all the shades of selfies in the prior categories.**

> ➢ **Play with your friends and see which category they come in.**

➤ **Do the Challenge and see if you can get most of the selfies ticked off the bucket list and challenge your friends as well. Or create your own bucket list. It's totally up to you.**

To truly grasp and appreciate this guidebook you will need to look at your own selfies that you take and most likely send to others or put on Apps such as Snapchat or Instagram etc. Compare the different shades of selfies you have sent with the bucket list. Can you see a pattern from the types of selfies you take or send out constantly? If you send certain similar types of selfies more than others then you are more likely to find the category you fall under.

Now that you know all that has been revealed. You are more likely to understand and perceive a selfie for what it truly is.

THE POWER OF KNOWLEDGE

You have read this guidebook and perhaps you are ready to take things a bit further. You know the old say knowledge is power. **Use the technique I am going to reveal to you for your advantage. The power to manipulate and befriend a certain person for personal gain is about to be revealed.**

If you are a constant user of certain apps, websites or have many friends that send out plenty of selfies then you're in luck. You may even have people on your mind that you want to follow or have many people that follow you. You can use this guidebook for your own advantage as you understand that person better and you know what they are most likely to be like as a person. Or you can give out a better vibe about yourself by controlling the types of selfies you send out.

For your advantage I am providing you with some bonus information. You can use the method I am going to provide you to help you identify the traits of a person through their selfies. All you need to do is compare the frequency of a certain selfie and then use the formula to reveal that persons main traits.

The formula of different shades of selfies (identified by numbers from the list) to help you recognise a particular type of person is provided in table form on the next page.

Trait = A true friend – Can keep long term relationships	Trait = Have a laugh – Fun times
•7 •10 •11 •13 •16 •19 •29	•5 •11 •12 •22 •23 •27 •28 •30 •33

Trait = Available or looking – Boyfriend/Girlfriend	Trait = One night stand- Short intimate relationships
•8 •16 •23 •24 •25 •40 •45	•15 •36 •37 •38 •39 •40

Note: To qualify for the trait a majority of the numbers shown (of the different selfies) in the identified list in the table must be present.

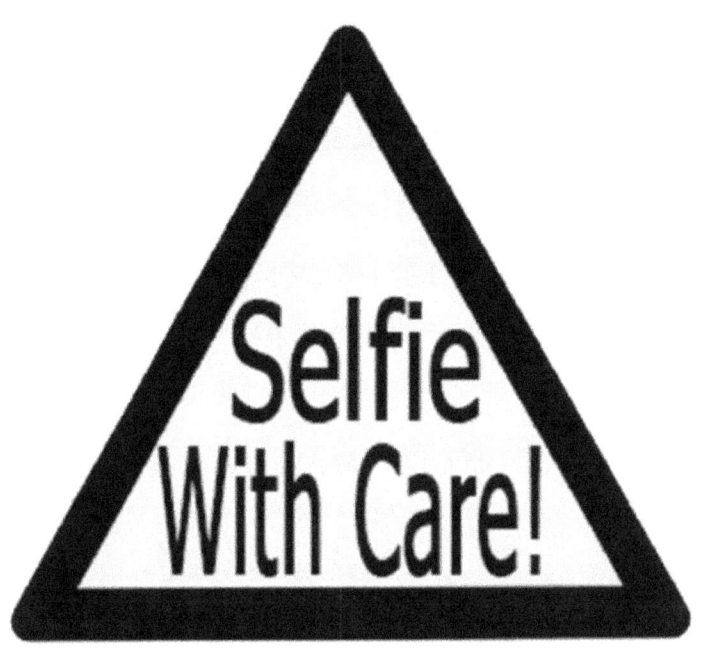

OTHER BOOKS BY SID ALI SABIR

Available Online at Amazon

WIZY EDDY'S MYSTIC 7: THE BOOK OF NUMINOUS – (BOOK 1)

WIZY EDDY'S MYSTIC 7 - MASTERING THE 7 – (BOOK 2)
Coming Soon

WIZY EDDY'S ? (SERIES)
Coming Soon

ONE LAST THING

If you enjoyed reading this guidebook I would be very grateful for you to leave a review. Your support really does make a difference and I read all reviews personally. Please visit amazon and search for the author or title and leave a review.

 If you have any suggestions or have spotted any errors then please email me at sid101@outlook.com so that I can make this guidebook even better.

Thanks again for your support.

www.ingramcontent.com/pod-product-compliance
Lightning Source LLC
Chambersburg PA
CBHW070422190526
45169CB00003B/1366